Early
Harvest

Early Harvest

Edited by Rachele Syme

Student Writing from The Rural Readers Project

Story Line Press
2000

Published by Story Line Press, Inc., Three Oaks Farm, PO Box 1240, Ashland, OR 97520-0055, www.storylinepress.com

This publication was made possible thanks to the generous support of the Ford Family Foundation, the Meyer Memorial Trust, the Walt and Peggy Morey Fund administered by the Oregon Community Foundation, the SURDNA Foundation and the Herbert A. Templeton Foundation.

Text Design by Rachele Syme
Cover Design by Lysa McDowell

ISBN: 1-885266-92-8

Library of Congress Cataloging-in-Publication Data

Early harvest : student writing from the Rural Readers Project / edited by Rachele Syme.
    p. cm.
    ISBN 1-885266-92-8 (alk. paper)
    1. High school students' writings, American--Oregon. 2. High school students' writings, American--Washington (State) 3. School verse, American--Washington (State) 4. School prose, American--Washington (State) 5. Washington (State)--Literary collections. 6. School verse, American--Oregon. 7. School prose, American--Oregon. 8. Oregon--Literary collections. I. Syme, Rachele, 1975- II. Rural Readers Project.

PS571.O7 E28 2000
810.8'09283'09795--dc21

00-0297909

This anthology is part of The Rural Readers Project coordinated by Story Line Press. The Rural Readers Project sends nationally published authors to high schools in rural communities throughout Oregon to promote literacy and the literary arts.

Participating Schools
&
Coordinating Faculty

OREGON

Enterprise High School, Enterprise
JENNIFER FRENTRESS

Center for Alternative Learning at Franklin School, Corvallis
MOIRA MCKENNA

Central Linn High School, Halsey
KEN BOLF

Crater High School, Central Point
VINCENT A. WIXON

The Dalles High School, The Dalles
TIM ZENKER

Elgin High School, Elgin
JANET SCOPES

Fresh Start Program at Corvallis High School, Corvallis
SHEILA SHAFER

Harrisburg Union High School, Harrisburg
DONNA PLUTH

Hood River Valley High School, Hood River
YOLANDE LAND

Opportunity School, Hood River
REVELYN RAWDIN, & MARY JANE SWANSON

Marshfield Senior High School, Coos Bay
OSKIE YASANA

Newport High School, Newport
JOHN HARRINGTON

Renaissance School, Eagle Point
KATHERINE LEPPEK

St. Mary's School, Medford
CHRIS JENSEN

Taft High School, Lincoln City
JOHN F. SOLLERS

Toledo High School, Toledo
PAM GILL

WASHINGTON

Port Townsend High School, Port Townsend
CHRIS PIERSON

Wallowa High School, Wallowa
JESS TURNER

PARTICIPATING AUTHORS

LEANNE GRABEL received her Bachelor of Arts in English at Stanford University. She has worked as a free-lance writer and editor for almost 20 years for a variety of local and national magazines. She has also published ten books of poetry, edited five poetry anthologies and received five regional arts grants for spoken word performance and publishing. Currently, Grabel works as a Writer in Education for Public schools, Literary Arts, Inc., and SmartStart in Portland were she resides with her husband and two children. Previously, she worked as a Trial Assistant and Client Liaison for the Metropolitan Public Defenders office. She enjoys working with "at risk" teens and conducting poetry workshops at MacLaren Detention Center. Mrs. Grabel also helps manage a small cafe known as Cafe Lena which she and her husband opened six years ago.

PATRICK KING has taught and tutored developmental and advanced English composition and literature at the secondary and college level. In addition to being the author of numerous stories and verse, which have been published in various literary magazines, he published his novel, *Son of a Buck* in 1998. Additionally, he was the recipient of the writing award for short fiction from the Cookeville Writing Association in Tennessee. At present Mr. King is a writing consultant for CitiCorp TTI in Santa Monica, California, as well as an English Instructor and Humanities Tutoring Coordinator at Santa Monica College in California. He holds a Masters degree in Comparative Literature, a Bachelor of Arts in English, and Associate Art degrees in Liberal Arts and Electronics Engineering.

The Rural Readers Project was the vision of ROBERT MCDOWELL, who founded Story Line Press in 1984 with his wife, Lysa McDowell, and Mark Jarman, a renowned poet and essayist. Since then he has worked as the press's editor and publisher. His poems, essays and stories appear in *The Hudson Review, Poetry, The New Criterion, The Kenyon Review, Poets & Writers, The American Scholar, London Magazine*, and *Harvard Review*, among others. McDowell has published three books of poems: *Quiet Money* (Holt, 1987), *The Diviners* (Peterloo Poets, 1995), and *The Pact* (limited edition, Aralia Press, 1996). He has taught at the University of Southern Indiana, The University of California at Santa Cruz, the West Chester Writers Conference, and the Writing Seminars at Bennington College.

CLEMENS STARCK'S first book of poems, *Journeyman's Wages*, (Story Line Press, 1995) received the William Stafford Award from the Pacific Northwest Bookseller's Association, as well as the 1996 Oregon Book Award for Poetry. His second book, *Studying Russian on Company Time* (Silverfish Review Press, 1999), was a finalist for the Oregon Book Award in 1999. Starck's third book of poetry, *China Basin* is forthcoming from Story Line Press. He has taught at Willamette University, and his poetry has appeared in a wide variety of publications, including *From Here We Speak: An Anthology of Oregon Poetry* and *Paperwork: Contemporary Poems from the Job.* He lives in Dallas, Oregon and works as a journeyman carpenter at Oregon State University in Corvallis.

JOHN TAYLOR was born in des Moines, Iowa, and has lived in France since 1977. He graduated *summa cum laude* from the University of Iowa with a degree in Mathematics and attended the University of Hamburg in Germany where he studied philosophy and German literature. *The Presence of Things Past* (Story Line Press, 1992) was his first collection of short stories, which was followed by a sequel of short stories entitled, *Mysteries of the Body and the Mind* (Story Line Press, 1998). As a regular contributor to *France Magazine* and *The Times Literary Supplement*, Taylor is considered to be one of the most knowledgeable and attentive critics of contemporary French literature.

TABLE OF CONTENTS

Center for Alternative Learning

Central Linn High School

Enterprise High School

Fresh Start Program

Harrisburg High School

Marshfield High School

Newport High School

Opportunity School

Taft High School

Story Line Press is proud to bring you the third volume of *Early Harvest*, a book that displays the fruits of The Rural Readers Project. Rural Readers was established five years ago by Story Line's Publisher, Robert McDowell, in an effort to expose high school students, especially in rural areas, to contemporary literary art and the artists who create it. Throughout the years, The Rural Readers Project has sent national authors of fiction and poetry to schools in Oregon, Arkansas and Washington to conduct writing workshops and to speak in rural communities about their experiences and expertise as writers.

In this year's anthology, readers will witness a colorful spectrum of styles and emotions. Students from Oregon and Washington present poems and prose of realization, fear, questioning, wisdom, unrequited love and appreciation. There are also sobering yet poignant words addressed to parents and peers, heartbreaking accounts of personal struggles, commentaries on social conflicts and political issues, playful depictions of lands of mirth as well as painterly descriptions of the sights and wonders of this world. These young minds present a veritable plethora of creativity that demonstrates the intelligence and insight of today's youth.

I would like to thank Story Line Press for giving me the opportunity to administer The Rural Readers Project and edit this anthology. I would also like to thank all the teachers who participated in Rural Readers, for their support and their belief in the importance and magic of the literary arts. Furthermore, I'd like to thank all the talented young artists who contributed their masterpieces. Although not all of the work submitted was published, each piece was carefully considered.

In addition to all of the participating authors, teachers and students, Story Line would like to extend a heartfelt thank you to The Ford Family Foundation, The Meyer Memorial Trust, The Peggy Morey Fund administered by the Oregon Community Foundation, the SURDNA Foundation, and the Herbert A. Templeton Foundation without whose support The Rural Readers Project would not be possible.

We look forward to tasting the fruits of next year's *Early Harvest* and reaping future crops of aspiring writers.

Write on!

RACHELE SYME
Editor

Story Line Press will carry on the Rural Readers tradition by sending writers to rural schools every school year. If you are interested in scheduling a Rural Readers visit at your school, would like to request more information about this project, or make a tax-deductible contribution, please contact Story Line:

Story Line Press
Three Oaks Farm
PO Box 1240
Ashland, OR 97520-0055
541-512-8792
541-512-8793 fax
www.storylinepress.com
mail@storylinepress.com

NO RESPECT

Some people can be quite annoying at times,
Talking as loud as can be.
Not just simple conversation,
But gossip about you and me.

They have no respect for teachers,
Or people trying to do the best work they can
They are annoying, rude and distracting
Though I really never doubted they would.

I do not respect these people,
They ruin all days that pass,
And everyday I hear them,
Wishing they weren't in my class.

Are they so blind not to notice,
The things they do each day?
To aim hate at other people,
 Just because things don't go their way.

These people try to be my friends,
But I just can't let that be.
Whether hurting friend or teacher,
Inside they are hurting me.

~ HOLLY PURDY, Center for Alternative Learning ~

TRUST AND YOU'LL BE TRUSTED...

Trust and you'll be trusted,
Said the Liar to the Fool,
"Do you believe in forever?"
"I don't even believe in tomorrow,
The only things that last forever
Are memories and sorrow."

~ JEREMY BRANHAM, Center for Alternative Learning ~

THE SUN

Outside everyday
Just sitting and staring for hours at the bright shining sun.
The grayish clouds covering the bright rays of light
multiple times making you squint to see anything.
Then you look away in blindness trying to focus on
something still trying to regain your vision.
Then the warm beams of sun warming your red rosy
cheeks, warming your body at the same time.
Then after a while the sun starts to go down, starts to get
chilly outside, then you decide to go in the house and you
think to yourself, 'Tomorrow the same thing!'

~ RIKKI BETTELYOUN, Center for Alternative Learning ~

KOSOVO

I can feel the hate surrounding,
Making tears that seem a shouting,
Lightning strikes of bombing flashes,
With human hearts comin' a crashing.

It can confuse the wisest of men,
With constant undeniable discontent,
In a world filled with hate we need
People who aren't ashamed.

To speak out above the pain,
Shouting words with disdain,
Clearing out the webs of hate,
And seeking resolution in this day.

For it can plague the soul and starve
The brain, sadly war is all the same.

~ LIZZIE WALTERS, Center for Alternative Learning ~

The smell of the rice began to fill the small trailer, as the rice cooker began to work its magic. The old woman took a seat now, resting her arthritic feet. She dusted the white flour from her gray hair.

"Grandma Susa, you must tell the story of the purple cloth!" she cried with much excitement.

"Haven't you heard enough of that tale?" The girl's mother scolded as she entered the kitchen while gently rocking a baby in her hands.

"Of course not. Well I'd almost completely forgotten it!" Her mother rolled her eyes at these words while handing the sleeping baby to his grandmother.

"Please Grandma, for the new baby. Please!" The granddaughter's eyes stared wildly in hope. Grandma Susa looked at the silent child and nodded her head.

"It was early morning when it was complete," she began, rocking the baby back and forth. "The lark was singing from a high branch as the sun arose over the village. She stood up and held it in great delight. The cloth encircled her fully, sticking out only where the child grew.

"It will do nicely," she thought.

The warm cloth shone in the early morning light, showing all its splendor. The purple glistened and the embroidered pink flowers projected upon the wall of the house. A gust of wind waved the silken blanket like a Japanese fan on a hot day. Worrying she might lose her hold of it, she neatly folded it up and placed it into a linen chest. Looking out into the sky she realized she must prepare the morning meal. She hurried over to the cooker and opened it. Taking out the now dried rice she rolled it gently being sure to savor each grain. She then put it on a plate, along with a small cup of soy-sauce and carefully balancing it slowly walked to the sleeping room.

Once in, she placed the meal on a small side table and opened the blinds. After doing so she knelt and whispered into her husband's ear.

"Awake my husband, it is time to wake up."

He turned to the opposite side, giving the signal that he was indeed awake. The woman, seeing this, left the room.

After the morning meal she showed the cloth to her husband. She waited for a reply, but receiving none went on with her daily duties. Once out of sight of his wife the husband stood. Picking up the silken blanket he rubbed it against his rough face.

"Yes," he thought to himself, "this will do well for my first born son." And with that he placed the blanket back into the linen chest and returned to his rice.

The light on the rice cooker turned bright red, and Grandma Susa saw this. She gave the now awake baby over to her daughter and proceeded to open the top of the cooker. The steam from the cooked rice fogged her glasses as she scooped out handfuls of rice. After getting the supply needed she closed the lid. Taking the tray over to the table she pointed to the rice.

"I cannot roll rice and tell a story at the same time." She said looking into the eyes of her granddaughter.

"I will help!" she yelled, jumping from her seat. Grandma Susa nodded her head, showing approval and picked up the baby from the rocker.

"The baby came," Grandma Susa continued. "But it wasn't what the father expected; the son he had hoped for was not to be. A girl was given to the couple.

"How can this be?" said the new father. "I am cursed with a girl and a war at the same time! At least with a war a man has the chance to be honorable." And so on the day of his first child's birth the father was enlisted in the fight against the Americans in World War II.

With the husband at war all the new baby and mother could do was pray and wait. And so they did, every night they would pray for his safety and his return to them. And each night baby O Schichi slept with the purple cloth, receiving the love and warmth that her father could not give.

One day in the service mail a package came for the man. He tore it open frantically with his cold hands. Inside lay the purple blanket. As before he rubbed it upon his face. The silk ripped on the unshaven beard that had been left uncared for these many years. A spark of anger lit through his body.

"Why has my wife sent me this?" He said tossing it to the ground. "The child needs this more than I. O Schichi," he said with great pain upon his heart. "The one I've never held. I call myself brave but I have not even the courage to face my own daughter."

Peering down with damp eyes he noticed a letter at the bottom of the box. He picked it up and stared at it for a moment, almost too afraid to open it. Finally, his shivering fingers opened the envelope. Retrieving the letter he began to read:

Most Honorable Husband,

I know not if you will receive this letter, and if you do it will most likely be three weeks after I write these words. I hope you are well. I bring you sad news. Our child, O Schichi, has passed on. There was an American raid a few days past. The town was destroyed and as O Schichi and I ran, She tripped upon a stone. All has been taken care of. I spread her ashes over a life tree.

I only wish you had known her better. Many say she was like a firework, leaving colors of love and joy to all who held her. My mother described her as the most well-mannered four-year-old she had ever seen. When she was alive, I told her of you and how honorable you are. She loved hearing of you. I explained your leaving to fight for your country. She was especially proud of that.

We prayed for you every night; I still do, and I am sure she watches over both of us. Every night, when we finished praying for you she would kiss this blanket. On one such night I asked why she did so. She explained to me that she was going to send it to you, with a million kisses. She wished for you to have it so that you would keep warm.

So keep warm my husband and return to me.

Your Faithful Wife

Simply a husband now, he dropped the letter. Picking up the purple cloth he wrapped it around his body. "If only I had understood," He said out loud. "If only I had understood."

Grandma Susa paused now, looking upon the new born baby. She handed him to its mother and stood up. Disappearing momentarily, she returned with a purple cloth. The sun shown on it from the small trailer kitchen window, projecting the pink faded flowers. The mother holding the sleeping baby opened her arms widely so Grandma Susa could wrap it around her. After doing so she said, "After the war this blanket warmed me, and did so for your mother and big sister, and now for you." She paused for a moment, gently taking the child into her arms, "So keep warm little Richard, keep warm."

~ LIZZIE WALTERS, Center for Alternative Learning ~

PRIDE

It's the color of the sky on a clear, crisp day
Oozing with the sound of joy and happiness.
It has the shape of a green leaf,
It shines with beads of water as if it had just rained.
In it's hand it holds the world, calm and peaceful,
But all too confusing at the same time.
It sounds of words that you always want to hear,
Making you happy and warm on the inside.
It's mother, all the sweet things of the world
And its father, all the hard work and determination that
Will get you far in life.

~ SEMELE BAIR, Center for Alternative Learning ~

STRESS

Pop goes the kernel,
Pippy, pippy, pop, pop
My head's like a kernel that
Just won't stop.
Round and round it goes
It gets real hot.
'Cause my kernel ain't a kernel
Without butter on top.

~ DUSTY SUGDEN, Center for Alternative Learning ~

On a cool park bench in
the middle of fall, leaves
floated all around.
A young girl sat simply
watching as each one
touched the ground, but
there was more upon her
mind than golden leaves
or rain and though she
was feeling empty inside
her heart was full of pain.
And as the memories flew
through her mind
she decided she'd been hurt
for the very last time. So
she closed herself up
good and tight just as the
day turned into the night.

~ KRISTIN APPELT, Center for Alternative Learning ~

The Sun Motel. Have fun at the Sun Motel. To pick up my aunt for the funeral. Down from Washington with her two girls and her new boyfriend. I have never seen him. I will call him Jake. Congratulations, he's 25. I can tell you right now he couldn't take a training wheel off a bike but he sure can light my aunt's cigarette for her. Room 24, like the Spanish woman in the moustache told me. The door was (how textbooks would say) slightly ajar. Peering at me through the shadow of the little $44 a night room are two nervous eyes framed in yellow, broken hair: "Kim?" She did not seem to hear me say her name. She opens the door and the light lays its body onto hers. Oh, don't think of those high school portraits I have of her stuffed away in a box where I can easily retrieve and eye them. That long sand-colored hair, those white teeth! One never saw such a California girl! One never saw such a desert child.

Jake asks me for a jump-start. I dart out of the doorway to move my car. Kim watches, one frayed sock crossed over another. She stands on two baby doll shoes. She holds the long cigarette in her right hand, like a torch in the timber town breeze. An antenna sensing everything that she can't. She picks at her face with her left hand. That skin! When did California die? Where? It's not Washington's fault your dress is too small. Her leather jacket seems warm but hardly seems comfortable. The thick black swallows her whole.

I wasn't sure whether to be relieved or frightened not to see the girls. Jake gives me a goofy laugh, "I need gas - that's the problem." I tear the cables out. I take his gas can and Kim to the Fast Gas that seems to take forever to get to. I knew the girls had to be with their grandmother. Kim rubs her eyes. Sniff, cough, scratch, pick , drag, blow, hem hem — "So...how are you?" I drive. This long wide road in a timber town ruined by heavy trucks. I answer her question with a question seeing that it's perfectly obvious that *I'm* okay fully clothed and driving a Subaru '91 with a full tank.

I buy her coffee. She complains about her allergies.

My mother's sister. I look at her. Does she really love her girls? We meet them at the Micky D's. Susan, little Susan with the temper tantrums tries to cover her torn nylons. Amber is embarrassed. Kim wishes she hadn't left her cigarettes with Jake, who didn't want to come to the funeral and stayed at the café, which doesn't exist. I tell Susan the torn tights have character and I buy her breakfast.

Funeral time. I go through the motions and keep a calm and pleasant face. Looking at all my cousins, uncles, and great-aunts: she hit me once, he's held up well, where are her children? I thought he died... I find comfort in the one relative I'm not blood related to. My grandmother's second husband. My only grandfather. Here to help with the girls and his wife's grieving. Must be tough to lose a mother all at once. I lose mine only a little every day. My brother's wife nervously shakes my hand. My face painfully holds a comforting smile that she doesn't seem to notice. I find a new face in the sea of "Familiar." Great-uncle Joe Vaughngati. I knew we had more Italians in our family. Lenora Jordani, who poked and teased me as a child almost died there herself from shock when I called her name... She's so huge now, Aunt Lenora, her face has grown kinder, her hair whiter. I hope to see her again.

The funeral alone fills enough thoughts in my head to fill a book. I guess that is what funerals do. Kim coughs. I click back into the old routine. I drive her back to the motel where Jake has packed their things. She speaks cruelly of the relatives. Aunt Caroline, who cried hysterically at the funeral, used to chase the poor children with a knife. Will she ever learn that cutting off a thumb will not stop a child's sucking habit? Kim shakes my hand and says that she is not "huggy." The girls wave from the back of the old station wagon as they head back north.

My grandmother's name was Crystal. My heart skipped a beat several times throughout the burying. "Here lay Crystal...In loving memory of Crystal..."

~ CRYSTAL ALEX HUFF, Central Linn High School ~

TOWHEES

There is a witch in my birdbath.
The stone gargoyle sits in it frozen and helpless.
She walks on his head and laughs in his face.
Her brown cloak flaps furiously as if casting damnation on his soul.
Others, like her, (though not as fierce) stand and watch.
Red eyes burn into mine. The mate has arrived.
He pushes his black head through the crowd.
One by one they take off.
He picks at the dirt then looks at me callously.

Chewink! Chewink!

I thank the window separating me from this evil.
The male demands his brown beauty to leave the
        stone man be.
Together they stop my breath. I feel a little sad.

These two twins from the ancient trees now rummage
noisily among dead leaves.

~ CRYSTAL ALEX HUFF, Central Linn High School ~

THE SUN FELL SWIFTLY BEHIND THE HILLS...

The sun fell swiftly behind the hills and a chilling phantom
    sweeps across the land.
You cannot hear it, for it makes no sound.
You cannot see it until it is already gone.
Yet you know it is there, you can feel it, you can see the changes
    it has brought on the earth around you.
Silently it blows across the sparkling dew,
A quiet river of silver-white frost is all that remains in its
    flowing path.
Swiftly it hits the streams and ponds,
Shimmering with ice they stand, like glassy mirrors in the soft
    moonlight.
Gently it nips at the bare parts of my skin,
Causing shivers down my spine as if my blood were frozen solid
    with the night.
Softly it leaves,
With the rising of the sun and the promise of a new day.

~ BIRCH BARREN, Central Linn High School ~

FLIGHT FROM WINTER'S WRATH

The breeze whistles
over abandoned cliffs,
with nary a man to mind it.

Here the clouds gather
delivering cold rain and a dark sky
as well as a message,
a message meant for winged divinities,
for birds.

The sky turns a crimson red
a storm-filled twilight,
and so the birds follow the wind
plummeting southward from the dawning
of the season of bitter cold and death
from winter.

~ OWEN LLOYD, Central Linn High School ~

THE STRANGER

The park,
always quiet,
always peaceful.
A day separated and remembered by a life-changing experience.
A stranger walked into my life,
changing it forever.
No words,
no motions of any kind.
But as this stranger passed he gave me a gift.
I looked into his eyes and there, looking back, was me.
Just for an instant was the knowing --we are all the same,
Just for an instant he was not longer a stranger,
he was a human
just like me.

~ TAMMY CORLISS, Central Linn High School ~

BURGER KING

Our favorite place to eat.
She orders.
I sit patiently watching cars drive by.
A static-strained-voiced waitress tells her to pull up to the window.
She grabs the sack from the static-strained-voiced waitress
And hands the sack to me.
I peer inside
The wondrous, mouth-watering dessert sits at the bottom,
Untouched,
Untasted,
Waiting,
As I examine the bag that holds this delicious treat,
I notice to my grief-stricken surprise,
There is no fork.

~ MONICA ROSE, Central Linn High School ~

LOVE

What hope is there
In living or dying
What hope is there
for this feeble form
        to know

We walk
and stumble
and crawl upon jagged rocks
We cry out at others
and blame them for our state

We reach up one torn
and bloody hand
Saying
"What now can be done?"

We are lost
And cannot see
That the darkness
Has long since passed away

And these hands
That we raise up in anger
These stained and tortured hands
Are weeping for the deeds we
        make them do

And perhaps
We are just weary travelers
        passing through

Clinging to the road
Scared of being washed
    away like insects

So I ask you
What hope is there
When all we want
    is relief?
What hope is there?

~ BENJAMIN PURKERSON, Central Linn High School ~

Cancelled. It's amazing how eight little letters can change your mood in a matter of seconds. After studying the many destinations, arrival, and departure times, I was sure there had been a mistake. Defeat sank in, and I turned away from the glowing screen. A wave of disappointment, almost sorrow struck me, knowing that I would miss spending Thanksgiving with my parents in New York. As I walked down the hall, I suddenly realized that the floor was deathly cold. The white tiles chilled my feet through my new wingtips. Being abandoned in an airport, let alone in Minneapolis, wasn't exactly how I had planned on spending my Thanksgiving. As I carefully selected a padded chair nestled in one of many rows, I found the falling snow outside of the windows dreary, and depressing, and instead chose to sit where I could watch the people. My black trench coat, and maroon scarf gave me a sense of security. I soon let my dismal mood drift away with the steam coming from my cappuccino and became enveloped in the constant bustle of the people passing by. I chuckled to myself as I quickly made the distinction between the mothers who had well behaved children, and the pitiful mothers dragging the little devils as if they were on a leash.

"Don't touch that, James! Would you hurry up, Bri! Don't hit your sister!"

After thanking God for not having such quandaries, I noticed a great deal of reunions carrying on. Two sweethearts barely out of college embraced just outside Gate 32, a bouquet of marigolds and baby's breath clutched in her left hand. I also noticed an elderly man in an old wool sports jacket, struggling to balance two coffees and a large muffin, while cradling this morning's *USA Today* under his arm. He was careful with each step, and I found myself watching him for some time as he slowly made his way down the long hall. Feelings of peace and tranquility surrounded me and I was surprisingly content, considering my situation. 'How often do I get time to myself?' I pondered. Realizing that worrying and becoming frustrated wasn't going to make my predicament any better, I decided to take in the moment, and slowly drifted off to sleep.

~ RYAN PACE, Enterprise High School, Jr. ~

PANIC

Small and huddled, I can't see who walked in.
My mother? My sister? My friend?
Panic rises in my stomach like it's alive.
The color is black, everything is black.
Even though my torment is too, I can see it through the black,
    colorless, but colored.
I can smell the salt and taste it in the back of my throat.
It's like I'm trapped.
It holds out its crumbled hands, they look like they are filled with rocks,
    gnarled and lumpy.
I know that it's a she, 'cause I know.
Her hands are cold; they cut right through me.
Her mother's Chaos , her father is Guilt.
She whispers so softly, but the tears trickle down her face.
So then I was wrong and she whispers again.
It's blown from my ears and lost to the wind outside.

~ NORA FRANKLIN, Fresh Start Program ~

STUPIDITY

I look behind me at the door.
As it opens Stupidity walks through.
Its clothes were colored in a mixture of yellow, green and orange.
It was happy, not embarrassed by its appearance.
It had the smell of cheap cologne.
In its hand it had three juggling balls,
As if it appeared it was trying to act silly instead of stupid.
Its mother was a drunk and its father was an abuser.
It looked at me and said,
"Help Me"

~ ANDY DUNSBERGEN, Fresh Start Program ~

PITY

Everyday I look out a window.
Everyday I see Pity.
I see it deep within.
I feel it as they walk by, like a lady on a corner in a short dress.
To her she's no good; Pity is too big.
It swallows you whole leaving no room to move.
You scream for help, but there's nothing you can do.

~ GEORGE BROWN, Fresh Start Program ~

POETIC DEFINITIONS

"I define poetry to be a collected piece of writing that has in some form a connection throughout. Sometimes the connections aren't extremely defined, but they are there, in some fashion connecting the lines."

~ GREG EICKMEYER ~

"Poetry can be the manipulation of words and/or phrases to form abstract pieces of writing. Poetry is often imaginative and comes from the hopes and dreams of the writer. Poetry can flow calmly and steadily like a mountain stream, or it can crash and break like the ocean against a rock cliff. Poetry may tell a story or make a point. Poetry can be a jumble of words simply thrown on a sheet of paper with no apparent relation or reason. Poetry is anything the author makes it."

~ HOLLY CULVER ~

"Communication of thought and feeling in concentrate form; just add thinking."

~ NICK REISER ~

"A medium in which one can express one's feelings or mind set on paper for others to read and/or puzzle over."

~ ROBIN RANIT ~

"How would I define poetry? I'd have to start by saying, poetry is an expression. Maybe not just one, but several. It's emotional. It's love and hate and passion, sometimes all at the same time. Poetry helps me express my feelings when I write it. It's a way to relieve tension and stress. I love poetry. Reading it makes me happy. Sometimes it makes me sad though, too. It is love and passion and pain and pleasure. It just simply is...an expression."

~ CARRIE TUCKER ~

"To me, a poem is very special. It is words given to explain a feeling, a very difficult thing to explain, or words weaved together in a beautiful way to bring clear a moment or a memory or a thought. These words usually are put together with a lot of skill, for they have a musical quality to them when read out loud. Just the thought of bringing simple words together in such a precise, and at the same time random way, that it can capture a moment in a beautiful and very original way, inspires me. The possibilities of poems then seem endless when I think of what they really are."

~ MELISSA BELLINGHAM ~

"What is poetry? Poetry is putting into words the things you are feeling. Poems can be happy, sad, funny, serious, whatever, but whatever they are, they come from within...."

~ RON ROGERS ~

"I feel poetry is just an arrangement of words used to convey someone's emotions in a situation. I use poetry to vent when I am very emotional. I often see other aspects of people and their experiences through poetry. I get introduced to ideas that never occurred to me before. I get to feel what others felt, to picture what they saw. It's like letting someone inside your heart for a minute...."

~ ANNIE CARUSO ~

~ EICKMEYER, CULVER, REISER, RANIT, TUCKER, BELLINGHAM, ~
ROGERS & CARUSO, Harrisburg High School

I don't know how it happened. I don't even know why. But ever since it did, I have begun to do things that I never even dreamed of attempting before. Take this, for example. If I wasn't invisible I would never have had the courage to sneak into the faculty lounge. I wanted to see what went on in there, but I never had the guts to try and enter. But now that no one could see me, I was perfectly safe. Still, it felt weird to actually be standing there, waiting for the door to open so that I could slip in. The door was always locked. Without the key, the only way in was to wait patiently until somebody else left, and then slip through the opening before it closed again. I remember the last kid who tried to sneak a peak into this room.

It was right after lunch and somebody had dared him to get in and then take a picture. There was a bet of $75 if he completed the task, so he was all for the mission. I remember him making it up to the door but not much past that. He started to pull the handle, to test and see if it was locked, and right then the principal came out the door, grabbed his ear, and pulled him into the office. We heard he was expelled but nobody ever heard anything about him after that. That episode only raised the suspicions of the room. He was the first and the only person that ever attempted to penetrate the teachers' lounge door until now.

I figured that I had quite the advantage since nobody could see me. I could slip in and out, undetected. Nobody would ever have to know. Just then Mr. Watson left the room and I seized my opportunity. I slid through the door just as it was beginning to close and easily entered the room. When I first walked in I was so excited that everything just looked like one big blur. But as soon as the room started to take shape my excitement plummeted. There was absolutely nothing spectacular or odd about the room. It contained only a large wooden table, a dozen orange chairs, and a banana yellow, vinyl wraparound couch. There were only four teachers in the room at the time; two were sitting on the couch, reading and grading papers, and the other two were lounging in the chairs, drinking coffee, and sharing battle stories about their day. I was, needless to say, quite disappointed with my findings, so I decided to crawl up on the fridge and wait awhile.

I had spent about an hour and a half up on top of the fridge, and I was just beginning to doze off when dozens of teachers started to enter the room. In no more than five minutes, every teacher at the school had congregated in the lounge. Some of them pulled up a chair around the table, some sat on the couch, and still others leaned up against the wall. Now I was interested. From where I sat I could observe all of them, talking in hushed tones to each other, glancing around to check for intruders. They stayed that way for about ten minutes until a man I had never seen before called the meeting to order. At first they started by talking about grade reports, upcoming school activities, and other things commonly associated with students and teachers. However, then they began talking about "the project." The new man who everybody called Captain Throttle asked questions of each teacher about their progress. All the teachers responded that everything was working out great and that they hadn't come across much resistance. The meeting went on for more than two hours.

At the end of the second hour I was confused. I was getting ready to leave. I had no clue what this "project" was they were speaking of. Then Throttle unknowingly let me in on the secret. He outlined the plans for the teachers, giving them each a copy of a very complex looking packet. Then he summarized the entire project with one dramatic line. "Once we are done, the school food will be edible once more." I was astounded to say the least. All this time I though that they might be talking about some amazing project that would rid the school of most, if not all, of its blemishes. But the whole time they had been taking on a task that was impossible. To think that our teachers would join together and waste so much time on such an impossible task obliterated every last sliver of trust I held in the public school system. I left the lounge disappointed and tired. I headed out the door, jumped into my Caddie, and started home, hoping the rest of the day wouldn't be such a waste.

~ LORI WOLFARD, Harrisburg High School ~

She strode silently next to him
Feeling unacquainted in the cold, wet night
The young woman feels an urge to grab his big hand
Which she knows is always warm
Hers are cold but she can't tell him that
She wishes she was little
Never needing an excuse to be affectionate
Having to quicken her pace to keep in step
Watching him eagerly yet cautiously, then
She glances up into the big clear sky
For a brief moment things are simple
A small, knowing smile skips on then off of her numb face
She draws in some bitter air
And reaches for her father's hand

~ ANNIE CARUSO, Harrisburg High School ~

UNTITLED

Thick, dark clouds hung low in the early morning sky. Breaths of cold wind whispered threats of rain throughout the near-bare branches of the lonely trees. Blankets of soft white mist hovered in the hollows and ruts that indented the moist ground.

On a wooded hill, an intimate group of solemn people proceeded up a narrow stone path. The soft sounds of muffled crying drifted across the stillness of the hillside until it faded into the trees. A small, unkempt cemetery lay ahead of the group. Off to the nearest side was a small coffin, cheaply constructed, in which rested a child's body. Standing next to the coffin were two people — the mother of the child and the priest.

She was young. Not a day over 17, it seemed. Perhaps she was even younger. She was unusually tall for an Ecuadorian, but she was so thin and frail one hardly even noticed her height. Her hair was loosely held back with a dirty rubber band. Wisps of it, too short to be held, hung limply around her face.

Her face was shaped like a heart, suggesting the real beauty her face could hold. But her eyes were too old, her face too plagued by a year of constant worries to be beautiful.

She raised quiet eyes to gaze at the group of people that had gathered around. Her friends and relatives were saddened by her. Her face seemed to have aged overnight. Beneath her deep-brown eyes hung dark circles of weariness. The whites of her eyes glowed with a raw pinkish color that revealed the long night of crying.

Her cheeks had rid themselves of girlish blushes forever. Instead, her face held the drained color of a woman who no longer could see the world through a child's eyes. A woman forced, kicking and screaming, into this cold funeral procession, to bear it all and to bear it alone.

She shivered and wrapped her ragged black shawl more tightly around her bony shoulders, The priest's words washed over her in monotone waves of nothingness. They brought no comfort.

Suddenly a low moan of deep thunder rolled over the cemetery. Icy droplets of rain began to descend from the ever-darkening sky above. Quickly, the people scattered to the inadequate but only available shelter of an evergreen tree.

The people turned sympathetic eyes towards the mother of the child who was still standing in the rain. She was staring at nothing in a dead stupor. The rain pounded down in waves, beating on the tiny woman's body. Cheap jeans, with a hole in the right hip, and a dark brown sweater clung tightly to the soaked woman's body.

Abruptly, the woman lifted pain-filled eyes to the eternal bed of her one and only child. She unsurely took a step towards it and then paused, a look of wild fear crossing her face. In an instant, the look had vanished and swallowing, she went forward again. Her arms stretched out and she poignantly rested a limp palm on the wooden lid of the coffin. Tears and rain drops ran in confusion down her face as she slightly tilted her head to the side to stare at her child's fate.

She stood there for a long time. Sheets of violent wind and rain soaked her figure; lightning flashed angrily, full-toned thunder growled back, and still she did not move.

Then, something inside the youthful mother died forever. In place of what she had lost, a tiny spark inside her eyes ignited and new hope wove itself into her spine. Her eyes focused back on the coffin lid in front of her, and she stroked it affectionately for the final time. Then, slowly, she turned to face the raging storm that had pounded at her back, head on.

She stood erect; her back straight, her head held high. In her tiny form was inner courage that was now unmistakably concrete. She stood in the howling wind, almost challenging it with her loss of fear for what it could bring. Then she shrugged.

Slowly she reached behind her and pulled the rubber band out of her hair, shaking her head back and forth. Black, shimmering strands fell around her supple face. Her glistening head tilted backwards, and cold rain washed over her face in small rivers. She raked her slender fingers through her hair.

Then she heaved a great sigh, and turned her back on it all: the cemetery, the funeral, the few people that stood huddled under the tree watching her. She turned and walked, through the storm, away from it all.

~ MELISSA BELLINGHAM, Harrisburg High School ~

A bleeding angel
Suspended in air just out of my reach.
I cannot get to her to help.
I call for her, I motion her,
No use.
She floats with her head hung over, weeping
Tears fall.
Collect into a pile of perfect diamonds.
Why won't this angel let me help?
What is she waiting for?
Waiting
Waiting
What does she want me to do-
Wait here while she cries in pain?
That's not right.
I call to her again.
No effect.
Her chest,
Drenched in blood from a wound at her left breast.
She needs help.
"Let me help!" I yell.
She will not listen.
"Trust me please!"
I shout almost in tears myself.
She looks up into my eyes and tears roll down cheeks of perfect
        ivory.
Eyes close.
A flash of light so brilliant my inner mind lights up.
I try to regain my sight.
Look around and find myself alone -
Alone except for a pile of diamonds and a puddle of blood.
I kneel down.
Examine a diamond.
Pick up the rest.
Put them into my pocket and take them with me as I leave.
Those precious diamonds.

~ ROBERT BAILEY, Harrisburg High School ~

With a lantern that wouldn't burn, the old
farmer trudged out through the cold
Montana night. The snow crunched beneath
his boots as he made his way to the
barn to check on the restless stock. He
shivered as the wind began to pick up
and as it slipped inside his corduroy
coat collar. As the clouds drifted in front of
the moon, he wished that the flame in
his lantern wasn't so afraid of the dark.
The old man picked up his pace. Then
he heard it! The sound of a lone wolf
crying in the distance made the hair on the back of his
neck stand up. Oh, if only his lantern would burn!

~ ALISA BAKER, Harrisburg High School ~

A Piano, waiting to be touched by just the right hands,
Sits patiently, luring unsuspecting passersby to touch just one
   key.
Three people pass by and of these three, none of them are the
   right ones.
The day has been bright and sunny, making the piano's need all
   the more.
It is noon now, and the piano is growing weary of waiting.
The lounge has not been occupied for several slow hours.
Then, the door opens, and in walks the one, the right one, with
   the touch.
Gracefully, this person sits down, and begins to meet the piano's
   needs,
Taking it through Beethoven's fifth, and such songs as *Ode to Joy*,
   and *Morning Mood.*
The piano is happy again and laughs a new pitch as its player's
   fingers hit each key.
Even when the sunny day turns black and the rain begins to fall,
   it does not phase the piano.
It doesn't even phase the player, for that delight that the piano
   gets from the touch of a finger
Is the same that the player feels from the touch of a key.
The joy will soon end, but tomorrow brings another day of
   exploration for the piano, and me.

~ CARRIE TUCKER, Harrisburg High School ~

They sat there, staring at me.
I argued with them, they did not agree.
They talked on and on, not seeming to obey
For the purple Telletubbie was the topic of the day.
I told them, "Please don't cry."
They said to go get some shut-eye.
I did as I was told, because they were starting to grow mold.
When the morning came they were still at it
So I informed them about the purse and he was happy just a bit.
Then they told me that I must salute,
I laughed at them and said, "You are only fruit."
They replied, "Not just fruit but the best fruit of all."
And then they started to play baseball.
So then I left for school in the rain, leaving the orange on the
    wall.

~ Lori Wolfard, Harrisburg High School ~

HELLO YOU MIGHT SAY...

Hello, you might say, to an
Odd clown in your way.
Laughing, he would say, "Am I in your way?"
Leaping to his left, he clears a way,
You thankfully say, "Good-bye."

Cleverly following you he comes.
Under shadow and avoiding
Light, until he catches you by surprise.
Very cautiously this time you say hello, and he
Ever so slowly starts to go.
Reluctantly you turn and leave, but hear footsteps behind.

~ ELLERY WEBER, Harrisburg High School ~

Upon the floor there sat a stack
Upon the stack there sat a bee
The lone bee sat in a crack
On the stack of jubilee

All of a sudden my car ran out of gas
The painted surface I did breech
The scratch came out in the shape of a sash
Or was it the shape of a leech

The bee and I became very groggy
When the stack I did reap
The whole thing had become soggy
Suddenly I took a leap
The bee had become my lucky charm
And now it was time for him to disarm

~ HOLLY CULVER, Harrisburg High School ~

The girls laughed and piled in a stack.
The youngest one shrieked and yelled, "A bee!"
Her sister went to run, but tripped on a crack.
These times were sheer jubilee.

Happiness spread like a gas.
Our world could no one breech.
Joy a never-ending sash.
Reality a leech.

The giggling made us groggy.
Good times are difficult to reap.
But never a pillow to be soggy.
Our hearts can't help but leap.

Perfect memories never lose charm
And only love could ever disarm.

~ ANNIE CARUSO, Harrisburg High School ~

CHILD

I see a small child holding on.
To what I cannot tell.

There is fear here, inside.
It seeps from the walls.

That child is here.
In the walls, crying.

The wells went dry.
People beg for rain.

He's in that well.
He's still holding on.

His cry, the maddening sound.
He let go.

~ ERIC PERRY, Marshfield High School ~

CALL OF A CHILD

My dear mother. Are you ashamed of me?
Do you feel you messed up raising me?
Never forget.
You taught me how to walk,
Brush my teeth,
Fix my hair,
Laugh a little and cry.
You've taught me so much, mother.
Look into my eyes.
Tell me you love me.
My eyes are like yours.
If you lie to me... you lie to yourself.
Don't be ashamed, mother.

~ TIFFANY CROWDER, Marshfield High School ~

STAIRCASE

I dislike the taste of salt.
Warm saltwater in the corners of my mouth.
Saltwater that ran down my cheeks.
It came from my eyes.
You say my eyes are filled with hate.
But, I'm sorry sir, you're wrong.
Your eyes show disgust.
I do not hate you.
But, you are disgusted with my actions.
You want me to be the child you never raised.
You want me to be your good, Christian daughter.
What you don't see is that I am a good girl.
And, I am a Christian, too.
But, I am who I am.
That, you will not accept.
Now, sir, whose fault is that?

~ TIFFANY CROWDER, Marshfield High School ~

I thought my life was warm and full of friends.
We were all one big group. Girls with girls and boys with boys.
But nothing lasts forever, everything ends.
What happened to all those joys? She has no name, but she
      destroyed our lives.
Walked in, nitpicked on everyone, now she won't take the blame.
Why fix it? Nobody tries.
It's too late, we are mad at each other.
All because of her.
I try to be an open, honest, down to earth person.
Why do you stab my back with your betrayal knife?
Have you not learned your lesson?
Don't destroy our social life.
Nobody hangs out anymore, I feel so alone, as if I'm knocking
      and everyone shuts the door.

I do know a few good apples.
Those who have open ears and care to listen.
We stick together through all the trials.

Not worrying about their reputation, because we know what's
      right and how we feel.
Don't care about trying to please everyone but voice the real
      deal.
To those I have to thank, for they are the ones I call true friends.

I only wish that someday I would find true love,
But it seems as if it'll never happen.
What I seem to get in return is a big shove.
There goes my heart in an open sea, just drifting.
They say "my heart's not in it," no one's is.

I must not know how to deal with it.
But for right now, I don't care.
There is more in life to share.
Stop looking it'll find me.

Maybe I could forgive you for all the empty promises?
But, I think of all the things you've missed out on, and that's not
    my reaction.

Though I have been blessed with the best mother on earth.
I've never felt not good enough.
To her, I know what I'm worth.
I see the long neck bottles she's left
For me!
Can't you see?
She heals my wounds and kisses the Band-Aids.
She wipes my tears when I don't know what to do and need a
    shoulder's angle.
There is no way to know how to pay her.
God blessed me with an angel.

But through all the good and all the bad,
Sometimes I sit on this bed and look out the window.
Why am I so sad?
Maybe God's put all these hard, hurtful, but loving, happy
    emotions in my life
To make me a stronger person.
Maybe I'm just learning life's little lessons.

~ NORA HECKARD, Marshfield High School ~

A TRIBUTE OF HATE

A generation of repression lashes out,
Mindless zombies seek comfort in hate.
Loser, queer, freak, they are taunted,
A life of deception and therapy sessions.

Twisted reason creates truth from lies,
Forbidden prayers and naughty pleasures.
Darkness descends troubled dreams,
Devil's craft unleashes Hell's forces.

Young blooded vacant souls appear,
More young blood trapped like animals.
Irreligious inner strength takes action,
One gunned down with brutal sound.

Painstakingly mastered perfection tears flesh,
A second shot solidifies the kill.
Old friends never make the reunion home,
Few escape with flesh wounds or lush cuts.

Returning home, news of death impacts families,
An empty legacy of nationwide happenings.
A generation of repression seeks comfort
Laying down roses, a legend lives.

~ AMANDA ROSE, Marshfield High School ~

POISON

Poison in a book I read, makes the living see the dead.
Put my head down to the floor, and hear their tormented roars.
Quickly running back to bed, must be only in my head.
What could be behind that door, who is lying on my floor?

If I read by day, would it go away?
Would I be free at last, not to think of monsters past?
Might I be OK, will the images go away?
Thoughts come in so fast, they always seem to last.

Their imprints are permanent, to my mind they are sent.
In a black hole they are born, and from my mind they must be
        torn.
In my head there is a dent, and I am sure my mind is bent.
Prick my finger on a thorn, so poison will not take form.

Fainting from the sight of blood, I fall into the mushy mud
Will I ever fall again, surely it wouldn't be a sin.

~ DANICA JONES, Marshfield High School ~

FINKLESWINEWIPER WERTYWOHNSNIBBELDINGY JUNIOR: A HERO

There once was a man whose name was Finkleswinewiper Wertywohnsnibbeldingy Junior. This name may seem to be exceedingly bizarre, but let me assure you that the two people that so named their boy were, themselves, highly regular. Finkleswinewiper was not really brave and not very resourceful; he was not hero material, or a prime choice for much of anything, really.

Finkleswinewiper Wertywohnsnibbeldingy was the only son, and the only child at all, for that matter, of Bob and Sue Smith. The father (Bob) wanted to name his child Henry (as if there weren't enough Henrys in medieval times) or Bob the Second or some other manly name. The mother (Sue) insisted however, that their son would have a name that could be respected and looked up to in the courts of the land.

The man himself wasn't much to look at, other than his remarkably short legs, and torso, and neck, and — well, everything about him was small, if you bothered to look down and note the fact. When he was a child of ten years, the distance measured from his feet to the top of his head was the gargantuan length of three feet. When he grew until he would no longer grow, Finkleswinewiper grew to the majestic height of 3'4".

Now, by this time, the reader is undoubtedly wondering why, of any person who has ever been, I chose to inform the world that Finkleswinewiper Wertywohnsnibbeldingy once existed. This is a good question, which I will proceed to answer — but before I answer, I first need to recall a few more things about Finkleswinewiper's favorite things to do. Hold trust in the storyteller, for you will need to know these things.

Hobby number one: Wertywohnsnibbeldingy had an obsession with squeezing rare or exotic fruits. This may seem odd, but the greatest sages of the lands assured Junior's parents that it was a simple brain disorder, harmless, yet incurable. He couldn't help himself, in fact. Once he saw a fruit that he hadn't squeezed many times before, he had to squeeze it.

This compulsion of Finkleswinewiper's brought pity from some and sorrow from others (mostly fruit-stand owners and other market-men), but most often, people tended to laugh their heads off — not literally, of course, except for poor Mr. Crookhead Sidelside, who really doesn't belong in this story at all. People generally walked away or fell completely over in their mirth.

Hobby number two: Finkleswinewiper often went out alone and proceeded to crawl around near trees he could find, trying to capture small woodland animals with his bare hands. This allowed for a lot of contemplation time, which was aptly used.

Wertywohnsnibbeldingy was exceptionally good at his first hobby, not so good at the second. It was while performing this second hobby that I catch up to our Junior and begin to tell how he earned the title of "Hero".

Finkleswinewiper Wertywohnsnibbeldingy Junior was crawling around in the shrubbery of the forest known as Many-Overly-Large-Leafy-Trees, one day, when something peculiar happened. He was simply trying very unsuccessfully to capture small woodland animals when a very green and very scaly head poked out from behind a grove of overly large, leafy trees. This head preceded an equally green and scaly body, with large, pea-green, leathery wings.

Now, Wertywohnsnibbeldingy was not a stupid man. In fact, he was educated far more than what was good for him, for his long and sometimes silly-sounding words often caused him to be ignored (that and the fact that no one could see who was talking). Finkleswinewiper was educated enough so that he was able to name the creature that stalked towards him. It was a dragon, as you may well have guessed.

What really grabbed Wertywohnsnibbeldingy Junior's attention was the necklace of rotting bananas around the dragon's neck. Junior was immediately struck with a sudden urge to squeeze the bananas. He immediately began talking as if to a very young child.

"Here, little banunus...come and give me a huggy-wuggy!" The danger was greatly diminished in Junior's mind's eye. All he cared for was the squeezing of rare, exotic fruits, which the bananas were in that area of the world.

The dragon stood, just as the reader most likely would if you were in this dragon's position, very confused. The minuscule, unarmed man approached him, reaching out as if to embrace a lost love. Before the dragon knew it, the man had two arms as much around the scaly neck as the little man could put them. The little man was so small, he couldn't be scratched off, and he squeezed so hard and so long that he killed the dragon right then and there.

No one ever commented on the fact that Finkleswinewiper Wertywohnsnibbeldingy was only 3'4" tall... but then again, no one ever remembered him, either.

So goes the story of two fruit-lovers that met chasing woodland animals, one of whom found a rather embarrassing end, the other of which became the legend of Finkleswinewiper Wertywohnsnibbeldingy Junior, the Dragon-Slayer.

~ Chris Sifford, Marshfield High School ~

STONEHENGE

What are these massive stones we see
Their beauty not enhanced,
That rise above the ancient hills
And leave us so entranced?

Perhaps 'twas for celestial use
To trace a distant star,
Perhaps it was a meeting place
Of merchants from afar.

Did kings reside here pompously
A light in times so dark,
Or did the Romans storm the place
And seek to leave their mark?

Whatever use the stones once had
Remains a mystery
And ancient peoples of that land
Are locked in history.

~ HEIDI RICKEY, Newport High School ~

THE FISHERMAN

A cottage made of stone and thatch
A dory in the yard
A surly man with one eye patch
Is working very hard.

"Today I must repair my nets.
I see the weather turning.
I need some clothes, about two sets
Because the sea is churning."

To storms and gales and hurricanes
the man is hardly new
He's seen what harm and awful pains
An angry sea can do.

"Perhaps the sea's too rough today.
It's foolish to suppose
That just because I know my way
The sea will still repose.

"But yet the fish are calling me
And so I must depart
I'll tell my wife where I will be,
The keeper of my heart."

The woman begs the man to stay
But when a man decides,
His foolish pride will not be swayed
by violent, churning tides.
The little boat is turned and tossed.

The man inside does sway.
And when he feels that all is lost
The man begins to pray.

"Spare me, Lord, please let me live
My wife is on the shore.
Into my greed I will not give.
I'll go to sea no more."

The violent sea begins to die.
The man pulls in the bay.
The sailor who has just one eye
Is spared another day.

~ HEIDI RICKEY, Newport High School ~

My Sister:
dedicated to my older sister, Christi

We speak a secret language all our own.
The very best of playmates all these years.
And through the times of changes we have grown
Experiencing happiness and tears.

Remember all the stories we imagined?
We thought that we were mermaids in the sea.
We'd gather clothes and host a beauty pageant
And after that we'd have a spot of tea!

On summer days we always went exploring
To China or the center of the earth!
My early life could never be called boring,
Because you filled my youthful days with mirth.

But then one day you got a little older.
Your daily plans had changed so slightly then.
You started leaving home and getting bolder
With *other* friends who talked of trapping men.

You changed a bit because you were maturing.
My little mind could never comprehend.
Yet even then your love was so enduring,
Our love was something time could never bend.

Today we are so different, yet I wonder,
If make-believe has really found its end.
It's still the same old spell that we are under.
The magic of a true, devoted friend.

~ Heidi Rickey, Newport High School ~

PLANETS OF OUR SOLAR SYSTEM

MERCURY:
Hot and cold,
Yellow and white,
Mercury cannot make up its mind,
Scarred and rough,
Lava and ice

VENUS:

Hot, Hot, Hot,
Venus is yellow and hot,
Storms rage above and lightning crackles,
The surface is rocky and nicked,
I'd love to be there but it's just too hot!

EARTH:
Oh, earth is so lovely,
Oh, I am so glad to live on earth,
Oh, I am so lucky to live on earth,
Oh, I love earth,
Don't you?

MARS:
So red,
Like a giant apple in space,
It used to have life,
Like earth,
Maybe,
Maybe so,
Maybe no,
We will never know.

JUPITER:
Jupiter is very big,
It mostly just is gasses,

And not many land masses,
Actually not any at all,
It is very stormy,
And it has freckles.

SATURN:
Saturn has a big ring around it,
It sounds kind of phony but one of its moons is called phoebe,
17 moons in all,
Saturn is a lot like Jupiter,
It is a big magnet, too.

URANUS:
Blue it is,
Blue is it,
It has rings, too,
But they are vertical instead,
The gasses make it blue,
It has 15 moons.

NEPTUNE:
Gas, Gas, Gas,
A structure like Uranus,
And count them,
8 moons,
It is icy, too.

PLUTO:
Cold and small,
That is all,
But wait!
It has one moon,
Charon,
Some think it is an asteroid,
Others think it is a lost moon,
But we will never know.

~ HAGEN LAUBLE, Home Schooled, Opportunity School ~

WAVES

Waves crashed upon the beach washing away the sand.
Each time the waves grew higher,
thundering down upon the concrete wall,
smashing it into pieces.
People fled,
running down the streets like ants.
Buildings collapsed, crushing people.
The amusement park, washed away.
Many died, few remained.
Finally the movie was over.
Everyone who survived, left.

~ BRYNDEN RAWDIN MORRIS, Home Schooled, Opportunity School ~

Tornados are the dust
of sky god's chariots.
The deafening roar we hear
is the wheels grinding against the sky.
Behind them they leave a path
of destruction and chaos,
Even as the tiny mortals plead for them to stop.
The gods pay them no heed
for their minds are focused in another realm.
Clouds race across the sky,
spectators waving to their heroes
as the sky gods ride off to war.

~ LOEHN MORRIS, Home Schooled, Opportunity School ~

In the beginning it's small and clean. Purity shines through the untouched water. Growing with every inch, it flows steadily. Ahead occurs blind turns and past that, obscurity.

Approaching the first bend, there is no way to prepare for what lies ahead. The next stretch is turbulent and mad. The current sucks downward with such intensity there is no escaping. Here the water seems frigid and enraged. No longer clear, the water surges with swirls of grave brownness. Splashing violently against sable, flattened rocks, it swerves left and right, left and right until it seems to be going in circles. Furiously it flows around getting nowhere.

Struggling free of all its anger, the water winds narrowly through its shady spruce-lined path. The air around smells of freshness and of growth. Light shines through the prickly trees and teases the surface as it tiptoes along. Time ceases in this place of tranquility.

Another turn and the river becomes timid and frail. Once strong and powerful, it now trickles around stones to reach its final destination. Slowly it follows the path into the sea. The vivid sun sets emblazoned on the horizon.

~ TRACEY BEERS, Taft High School ~

LIFE

You might find
life is like chubby knees,
pretty much bad any way you look at it.

Other times you'll find
life is like a nice cold Dr. Pepper,
a simply beautiful thing.

~ JOE MOUNT, Taft High School ~

If you've ever loved and lost,
This poem is for you.
My writing's only opinion-based,
But all emotions are true.

A heart is like a bug,
It leads a happy life.
'Til someone comes and squashes it;
The pain cuts like a knife.

Love is a fragile thing;
It must be treated with care.
Others come along and tamper with it;
They do not play fair.

Blundering fools with all their lies
Will come and do you wrong.
Slashing away at your heart;
Causing your pain to prolong.

The heart can live with itself alone,
And most of the time it must.
Keep it safe from thieves and killers,
And most of all away from lust.

Your heart will break in future times,
But you must be strong
And if you're true to everything,
Then you cannot be wrong.

~ ELISABETH MORRISON, Taft High School ~

Fight for it.
You got it.
Burn it to the ground.
Pawn it off.
Don't claim it's yours.
Pool it up.
Make a collection.
Take it off.
Throw it away.
Knock it before you try it.
Peel it apart piece by piece.
Take it for granted.
Test it.
It's true.
Tear it apart limb for limb.
Rip it in half so it'll match all the others.
Touch it so gently, so beautifully.
Cut it too deep to heal.
Disrupt it deeply.
Bruise it.
Turn it black and blue.
Search through it.
You won't find anything you didn't know.
Use it for all it is worth.
Slam it on the table lifeless and limp.

~ GOLDA LOBELLO, Taft High School ~

ABOUT A LOOK

i have never had faith as i do for this
as i have for my love of you
yet a simple little thing
has shattered my faith
leaving seething anger, uncontained rage;
from along the cold hall
from across the bright room
a look is shared so that no one else can see
am i supposed to notice?
am i supposed to see?
something you said you felt for me
sent to another's eyes
betrayal without words
piercing my mind and life and soul
like a hundred barbed swords

every day my heart breaks
from a look across a room
it would seem to be true
so the bigger they are
the more painful the fall;
a forgotten tower crumbles at the sea
with less neglect, less agony
my love has shattered
a glint of an eye
a hint of a smile
my cold rage takes hold
jealousy and pain have taken over
a creature of pain is free
i rejoice in the release of pain
and i know i love you no more.

~ KEITH MILLER, Taft High School ~

AMOUR

This is a very precious thing.
It comes from the heart and it makes people sing.
We don't wonder about it.
We just celebrate it.

No matter the country, in France or in Spain,
We all understand it. The language is the same
We all want it,
But some can't have it.

We look for this thing wherever we go.
Did we miss it today? Will it come tomorrow?
We're all searching for it
But not all finding it.

It's as dark as any sea and as fierce as any storm,
Yet it's gentle like an autumn leaf falling in the light of morn.
Many things may seem like it,
But nothing is ever similar to it.

Consequence will never scare us away.
We'll go head on into it, come what may.
Friendship may lead to it.

With all the people 'round the world
Many faces, many names
This is the one emotion that makes us all the same.

~ AMANDA SMITH, Taft High School ~

VIOLATION

quiet hands
sneak over
her body
he says
it's their
little secret
her cheeks
are stained
with tears
her eyes
are closed
in fear
her body
lies frozen
under him
his hands
become angry
he grabs
and pulls
and scratches
his spit
and sweat
drip down
on her
he warns
her one
more time
and now
it's over
again.

~ ROSE MIGNANO, Taft High School ~

ROSE IN THE COLD

My grandmother says
we learn more from our failures
than from our successes.

Failure is delay, but not defeat.
It is a temporary indirect route,
not a dead end street.

The more a stone
is weathered by troubles,
The farther it will skip.

I remember this
When I made a mistake,
as if she'd planted
seeds of wisdom.

In my secret garden
a rose beams now
in the bitterest of cold.

I've learned not to agonize over my suffering
but to look for solutions in failure.

I hope I'm the one rose
in the woods of winter
so that later there'll be
dozens in my soul.

~ SIERRA KIM, Taft High School ~

IGNORANCE OR BLISS

The story —
and then the bliss is gone,
and one cares no longer.
Hide behind the armor of
ignorance,
replied I.

~ AMBER FOX, Taft High School ~

UN-

Unhappiness is a
Burden I carry
With glee, for
It gives me the
Strength to live
As I wish, and
To appreciate what
True happiness is
When I feel it.

~ KEITH MILLER, Taft High School ~

ALAS MY FRIEND...

Alas my friend;
I'll miss you much.
You've gone beyond;
All human touch.

I can hear
The sound of angel's wings.
For me it is an end;
For you a beginning.

You took the short way;
I strive to stay alive.
You let them beat you;
Now I must survive.

Past memories come rushing back,
But I'm forced to say so long.
I'm lost and confused;
My pain will prolong.

You left me all alone;
Alone to live a lie.
Why did you have to punish me?
Why did you have to die?

I'll always remember you,
Whenever I laugh or am in fear.
Now I'm leaving you with this,
A heart-filled, single tear.

~ ELISABETH MORRISON, Taft High School ~

WAITING FOR DAD

I look forward,
Through obstacles,
Through the pain,
Even through you.
I look past perpetual grief and shame.
For the moment
It is all that I can do.
Only yesterday I held your hand
And gazed in your eyes,
Unaware of what cruel fate had planned.
My hopes turned to lies.
Still I look forward,
Beyond the pain,
For the only thing my heart desires
Is the only thing it cannot gain.

~ HEATHER KINNEY, Taft High School ~

FEAR

I live my life
Scared from the dark
Boogie mans
Goblins
Monsters.
Everywhere I see
Their shadows.

They're under my bed.
They're in my closet.
They're behind my door.
I see them lurking
Waiting to come out.

But for now I am safe.
Safe from the terror.
Here in my bed
I am safe
Until night falls...

~ SAMANTHA SEARLES, Taft High School ~

THE PERFECT PICTURE

A colossal, teal-green wave crashed against the sandy shore, breaking against rough, protruding rocks and foaming like a newly poured root beer float. The sound echoed until the crash faded to a whisper. Again, a wave, littered with driftwood and sea shells, rose to the gods and angrily pounded on the helplessness below. With each wave that grazed the shore, the small, rounded pebbles tumbled farther in, spreading across the measureless landscape.

Seagulls soared overhead, seemingly stationary because of their defiance against the wind. Each bird's call, loud and uniform, poured from a bright orange beak like thick molasses.

Furious winds not only delayed the airborne animals: they lifted up clouds of sand, creating the illusion of an almost fog-like haze a foot above the ground.

Long, hairlike pieces of grass, arranged in clusters, blotted green spots on the otherwise brown earth. They flowed back and forth, waving good-bye to the passing birds, and, occasionally, they gave in to the pushing force behind them and broke.

Everything moved at a quick, hasty pace, but the fluid blend of all the different sights and sounds seemed to slow all the movement down. The waves seemed frozen in midair, their white foam not created yet. The birds were silenced by the awe of the landscape. The grass stood motionless as if it were afraid to move. The scene suddenly resembled a perfectly still picture.

Mr. Wilson stepped away from the fascinating picture, and he moved on to the next one. It looked as if it were an oil painting by Monet. "What an interesting museum!" he thought.

~ AMANDA SMITH, Taft High School ~

Hunger gnawed at her stomach as she stood near the front of the small store. Staring at the baskets of rolls displayed prettily just outside the store, her need intensified. The display looked exactly the same as it had when she had shopped there not too long ago. She stared at the golden crusted bread so intently she didn't notice her old friends shopping contentedly just inside the storefront's large picture windows. They would not have recognized her anyway. Outside, a young woman picked a round loaf out of one basket with her gloved hands. She turned it over, gave the bottom a tap, and listened to see if it was full of air pockets. Displeased with what she heard, she returned it to the basket and proceeded into the store. The gaunt, dirt-smudged female approached the baskets. The polished windows reflected what was behind her, but she didn't turn.

She focused on a young couple, hand in hand, strolling down the walk. The young girl wore a calico dress and had her hair pulled up off her tapering neck. He wore a pressed shirt with the button on the collar undone. In their free hands, he carried a picnic basket, and she held a red wool blanket. They were the king and queen of the picnic holiday. She was adorned with a tiara of daisies. He wore the crown jewel of a wild rose in his lapel. He was telling her a story about heroic deeds that he had done only in his fantasies. She gave a demure giggle and was proud to be seen with such a grand man.

They passed the windows, and all that was left in the emaciated woman's mind were the rolls. Crouching down so as not to be seen by the shoppers, she edged closer to the baskets. Slowly and carefully she dragged her knees over the cold pavement until she was looking over the edge of a finely made basket. Round, warm, golden nuggets smiled up at her. They basked in the evening sun and released an intoxicating aroma. Shaking her head, she came back to her senses. She darted a hand into the basket and came out with a feast fit for a king. She was reluctant to remove it from her sight, but it was just sitting in her hand, in front of God and everyone. She carefully placed it in a half torn pocket. Still on her knees, she backed away from the storefront. She rose slowly, making her back pain apparent.

Trying to hide her smirk of pleasure, she crossed the street to a small park. A vacant bench sprawled in the orange glow of the sun. She settled herself comfortably on the warmed boards. With careful fingers, she withdrew the pocketed treasure. It perched on her outstretched palm. She practically purred as she examined it. She raised it to her lips and with a rush of excitement took a trembling bite. It was the best bread she had in her life, her whole life. Memories of this life entered her mind like a swarm of bees. Each thought was sweet and satisfying, but not one failed to sting her soul. She saw herself, her friends, the baker... The baker who used to make loaves especially for her. He filled them with nuts and raisins and dusted the tops with confectioners' sugar.

What had she done? It hit her with full force. She had stolen from a friend. The bread turned bitter, and it crumbled into a coarse sand in her mouth. She sat stunned and bewildered. She was unable to reject the bread and unable to swallow it. She was stuck. All she could do was stare at that half eaten roll affixed to her hand. Slowly her gaze shifted upwards to the sun perched on the horizon.

It shone with the luster of the Aztec's gold, pure and beautiful. Quickly the hue changed to an unbecoming ruddy orange. The once optimistic sphere was pulled under the dark coverlet of earth with astonishing speed. In the black sky the absence of the sun left nothing but an even blacker hole.

~ JENNIFER FITZPATRICK, Taft High School ~

The gate clanks shut behind me, and I am home. A dove-colored pad of concrete lies under me and laps at the foot of the barn. Its summit smiles down on me and sends shadows sprawling across the sun-warmed ground. A sign, hand carved and brightly painted, is mounted high on a shingled wall. The etching simply and perfectly reads "Making Friends."

I enter the large, square cut door into the barn. My eyes are stunned from the contrast in brightness but adjust quickly to the shaded indoors. A satisfying coolness caresses my bare arms and face. The hairs at the nape of my neck dance and tingle with delight. I walk down the freshly swept aisle. Lines of missed dust cling to the concrete floor where the wide, well-loved push brooms were lifted and thumped before continuing on.

On both sides of me, stalls stand with doors open. Each stall has been filled with cedar dust that gives off a vermilion glow. The back of a broom has been carefully drawn across this bedding to smooth any divots left by the rakes. Only the tracks of tiny birds mar this velvet covering. A breeze that tiptoes through the barn carries the cedar's delightful perfume. I inhale deeply, and a smile slowly spreads over me.

I turn and walk to the front of a stall and lean against the solid timbers. A horse materializes out of my memory. She stands in the stall just as she had the first time I saw her. She stood tall with pride and held her head at a knowing angle. Her face was beautifully chiseled and distinctly feminine. Her well shaped ears were in constant motion as they scanned her surroundings. She stirred and took a lap around her new home. Her steps were long and powerful. I could see the muscles in her chest moving just under her skin. As she passed the small window, a stray ray of light hit her flank and reflected her bright auburn color everywhere. She came into the middle of her stall again and settled herself contentedly. I looked into her eyes. They were dark mahogany and as deep as mountain lakes. The deeper I looked into her eyes, the more I saw, until I saw directly into her soul. At that point I knew she would be mine. This memory fades just as quickly and unexpectedly as it had come.

Sun enters the open windows across from me and paints the window sills with its brilliance. The rays hesitate and then waterfall through the air landing in a pool of gilded cedar dust.

~ JENNIFER FITZPATRICK, Taft High School ~

THE WHALE

The bright, yellow sun rises up above the glowing, green hills, casting the sky into an illuminating glory. It is throwing blues, purples, pinks, and oranges into just the perfect plethora of colors as if to celebrate a new day's dawning.

Just beyond this extraordinary sky, and the glowing, green hills, lie thousands of gallons of flowing, moving, rippling water. The sun is casting its reflection upon the water, making it sparkle as if there are thousands of shimmering diamonds hidden beneath the surface.

Suddenly, without any warning at all, the shimmering surface shatters to reveal an incredible creature. Its body is jet black, with a white belly and two white patches on either side of its head. It is a killer whale who is performing magnificent acrobatics, which sends the water into a frenzy. It's as if the water is trying to escape the whale's performance.

Just as suddenly as the first whale appeared, six more long, brilliant, jet black dorsal fins standing high above the water appear. One of the whales jumps high into the air, and for a moment, looks like it will go clear to the sun. Just before the whale lands back into the diamond-studded water, the sun casts its shining rays upon the black of this beautiful creature, making it shine with a true radiance.

The whale crashes into the water, disappearing beneath the surface with the six other whales following close behind. The shimmering, glittering water returns to the exact state of calm that it had been in before.

~ ERIN BOSNJAK, Taft High School ~

94

In the early dawn the sunlight begins to rise above the hills. A thick layer of fog sits on the valley, smothering it, just as a pan lid does a stove fire. The newly arriving light illuminates the fog, making it glow in an eerie creamy white, like the inside of an Oreo cookie. Darkness melts from the sky, revealing a vivid sapphire blue, that becomes lighter with every passing moment. Yet, even though the darkness rapidly diminishes, three lights, Jupiter, Saturn, and Venus, penetrate the sky as if nothing will keep them from casting their golden light into the eyes of the world. A few clouds, looming above, appear marbled against the sky transformed into royal blue. They form decorative patterns that constantly change as they float along the currents of the air. The grass, which even in the early dawn stands out as a brilliant mint green, is saturated with water. Dew covers every inch of the blades of grass. When looking inside the droplets, it looks as if each one contains a whole new world trapped inside and yearning to be let out. The droplets are the same gorgeous blue as the sky as they reflect every image that the sky creates. They look as pure as the water in a watercolor painting.

The blue-black washes completely from the sky, and out of it explodes a dazzling turquoise. The brightened sky knocks the fading light from Jupiter and Saturn, but Venus remains in the Western sky, vibrant as before, throwing out pulses of lemony colored light. Venus shines like a lighthouse high above invisible rock barriers way out at sea.

The sky grows bluer. Eventually Venus fades away. The fog disperses and rises until it finally evaporates. Above the hills, the first yellow arc of our star can be seen. The sun is a buttercup opening its petals to the world.

~ ERIN BOSNJAK, Taft High School ~

Writing Without the Muse: 60 Beginning Exercises for the Creative Writer
By Beth Baruch Joselow

112 pages
$11.00 paperback
ISBN 1-885266-73-1

The Poem's Heartbeat: A Manual in Prosody
By Alfred Corn

161 Pages
$12.00 paperback
ISBN 1-885266-40-5

Story Line Press • Three Oaks Farm
PO Box 1240 • Ashland, OR 97520-0055
541-512-8792 • 541-512-8793 fax
www.storylinepress.com